Bentboy

Bentboy

Herbie Barnes

SCIROCCO DRAMA

Bentboy
first published 2024 by Scirocco Drama
An imprint of J. Gordon Shillingford Publishing Inc.
© 2024 Herbie Barnes

Scirocco Drama Editor: Glenda MacFarlane
Cover design by Doowah Design
Author photo by Cylla von Tiedemann
Production photos from the collection of the Centre for Indigenous Theatre.

Printed and bound in Canada on 100% post-consumer recycled paper.

Production inquiries to:
herbiebarnes@rogers.com

Library and Archives Canada Cataloguing in Publication

Title: Bentboy / Herbie Barnes.
Names: Barnes, Herbie, author.
Identifiers: Canadiana 20240358104 | ISBN 9781990738340 (softcover)
Subjects: LCGFT: Drama.
Classification: LCC PS8603.A758 B46 2024 | DDC C812/.6—dc23

We acknowledge the financial support of the Canada Council for the Arts, the Government of Canada, the Manitoba Arts Council, and the Manitoba Government for our publishing program.

J. Gordon Shillingford Publishing
P.O. Box 86, RPO Corydon Avenue, Winnipeg, MB Canada R3M 3S3

This story is dedicated to Leslee Silverman, who always made room for me and encouraged me—and so many others.

To Marjie, who lets me play and puts up with me, and to Andrew and Rebecca, who let me be someone I didn't think I would get to be.

Herbie Barnes

Herbie Barnes is an accomplished playwright, performer, director and arts educator whose thirty-year career spans stages across North America. He was among the generation of young Indigenous artists in the 1990s, breaking down barriers to forge professional careers in Canadian theatre.

As an actor, Herbie has performed in shows such as *The Hobbit, Children of God,* and *Cottagers and Indians.* Herbie has directed such classics as *Music Man, Oliver!, The Play That Goes Wrong,* and *Tales of an Urban Indian* in theatres such as the National Arts Centre, the Charlottetown Festival, and the Public Theater.

After working on other writers' projects for many years, Herbie started writing his own works. His plays include *Russell's World, Souvenir Alliances, Speak Easy or Else, Bentboy,* and *Father Tartuffe: An Indigenous Misadventure.* Herbie has been teaching for close to three decades at such institutions as Humber College, Sheridan College, and the Centre for Indigenous Theatre.

Herbie is currently the artistic director at Young People's Theatre in Toronto.

Acknowledgements

To Manitoba Theatre for Young People.

To Young People's Theatre and Allen MacInnis, for supporting workshops and guidance.

To Stephen Colella, who brought some words on a page to life and helped me find a wonderful story.

And to Paul Sun-Hung Lee, who inadvertently started this story over fish and chips at the Jason George.

Playwright's Note

Once I was playing Bilbo Baggins in a stage adaptation of *The Hobbit*. The production was good, and I think I was doing well in the titular role, but Gollum stole every show. In the book, the character was only in one chapter; in the paperback I read, that chapter was only five pages long—but what a character! My dressing room roommate remarked that someone should write Gollum's story.

I heard that, and being First Nations, thought, "What if I write the story of a young boy who could become a 'Gollum' if sent out of his community?" I wrote *Bentboy* thinking about what it means to be "broken" and what it takes to maintain positivity while being picked on by others, as happens to so many young people.

While developing this show, great adventure was what I was thinking about. Today, this journey might seem too difficult for young people to do alone, but great needs call for great acts... Or was this journey like my own, taken at age three, when I was determined to go to the local store under my mother's watchful eye, but got no further than the edge of my front yard?

Foreword

A few days before writing this foreword, I called Herbie to ask the most pressing questions facing anyone with a writing assignment: word count and due date. The conversation quickly veered to electric guitars; specifically, how many can one person reasonably own before it's deemed a problem, and the pros and cons of building one from a kit versus repairing cheap instruments found at garage sales. Herbie is a proponent of the build-your-own approach while I land squarely in the catch-and-repair camp. After the call, I couldn't remember if we had really addressed my questions, but I felt better nonetheless simply because I had been speaking with Herbie. A visit with Herbie, whether it's a phone call or in person, lifts my spirits regardless of what's happening in the world. It's not just that we would both rather talk about guitars than deadlines—it's the immediate and infectious enthusiasm with which he attacks the topic, illuminating possibilities that are sitting in plain sight, available to each of us.

Bentboy isn't an autobiographical play, but it's easy to see where the title character and Herbie overlap. Our hero, Bentboy, understands that there are challenges inherent to navigating the world and that he cannot waste his resources. By conserving his energy, he embraces the holistic management adage: *When I focus on the problem, the problem gets larger. When I focus on the solution, the problem goes away.* And even though he is the architect of his own disaster by falling in the creek and ruining his map, he doesn't dwell on this issue, nor does he waste precious energy by beating himself up. He continues to move forward while taking note of the world around him—nothing escapes his attention. His travelling companion, the brave and brash Hummingbird, repeatedly succumbs to exhaustion, while

Bentboy incrementally builds an inventory of knowledge and, by extension, a solution to each problem that they encounter. And very much like our playwright, he conveys these solutions with positive reinforcement, lifting Hummingbird rather than putting him down, just as the ancestors instruct us to do.

The premiere production of this script was fraught with the challenges of the COVID era. Actors lost rehearsal time due to the virus, auxiliary air-filtering equipment roared through the building, masks made it difficult to engage with each other, a major renovation to the theatre was behind schedule, yet everyone gamely stepped up to cover for each other and to accommodate the seemingly endless problems that all theatre artists were dealing with during those months of uncertainty. Throughout the process, as the director, I had the luxury of watching how each person embraced and deployed Bentboy's ethos of optimism and acceptance. This is a rare gift—to see and to feel the values and essence of the play take root, grow, and accelerate within the artists' practice.

The experience of working on this play holds an honoured position on the podium of favourite projects in my career. I raise my hands to Herbie and, in the language of my ancestors, offer him my heartfelt and lasting gratitude: Hóy7sxwq'e Si7ám.

Eric Coates
February 2024

Production History

Bentboy was first workshopped at Manitoba Theatre for Young People. The Centre for Indigenous Theatre presented a workshop production of *Bentboy* on May 12–15, 2016, directed by Ed Roy and starring Dale Alexis, April Bennett, Joel Chiefmoon, Laura Lee Lewis, Brendan Loonskin, Blaine McLeod, Jeremy Proulx, Randee Plain Eagle, and Sonny Russell.

A workshop with Young People's Theatre in Toronto led to a full production of the show in October of 2022, with Eric Coates directing. The YPT show featured the following cast and creative team:

Cast

Bentboy: ....Dylan Thomas-Bouchier
Hummingbird: .... Dillan Meighan-Chiblow
Eagleseye: ....PJ Prudat
Deerchild: ....Ashley Cook
Greyfowl: ....Daniel Yeh
Anonamouse/Tree: ....Brianne Tucker

Creative Team

Playwright: ....Herbie Barnes
Director: ....Eric Coates
Dramaturge: ....Stephen Colella
Stage Manager: .... Fiona Jones
Assistant Stage Manager: .... Kelsey Rae
Choreographer: .... Waawaate Fobister
Set & Video Design: .... Hailey Verbonac
Costume Design: ....Nishina Shapwaykeesic-Loft
Lighting Design: .... Shawn Henry
Sound Design: ....Keith Thomas
Auntie-in-Residence: ....Kelly Brownbill

Old Lady (April Bennett) makes sure the feast is a success. Centre for Indigenous Theatre production, 2016.

Eagleseye (Jeremy Proulx) introduces the village to the audience. Centre for Indigenous Theatre production, 2016.

Hummingbird (Randee Plain Eagle) is confused as to why he was not chosen over Bentboy (Jesse Wabigijic). Centre for Indigenous Theatre production, 2016.

The cast of *Bentboy*: Randee Plain Eagle, Laura Lee Lewis, Brendan Loonskin, Jesse Wabigijic, Jeremy Proulx, Blaine McLeod, April Bennett, Dale Alexis. Centre for Indigenous Theatre production, 2016.

Bentboy (Jessie Wabigijic) tries to explain why he doesn't feel lucky to Hummingbird (Randee Plain Eagle). Centre for Indigenous Theatre production, 2016.

Hummingbird (Randee Plain Eagle) and Bentboy (Jesse Wabigijic) realize the creek has grown into a river and might mean trouble for their journey. Centre for Indigenous Theatre production, 2016.

Characters

Bentboy
A young boy whose spine is as crooked as the creek but who has a good heart.

Hummingbird
A young boy who is popular and an example of what we think of as the "perfect" child.

Eagleseye
An elder who leads with their wits. Slow-moving, but by choice.

Deerchild
Someone who pushes others to do the uncomfortable tasks. Timid to talk out loud but will poke to get someone else to speak.

Greyfowl
A simple villager who follows a leader.

Anonamouse
The smallest voice of the village.

Tree
The oldest soul in the forest, with wisdom that transcends time.

Villagers, North Wind, Rocks, Clinging Vines.

Setting

A small village and surrounding forest. Pre-contact.

Production Note:

In future productions of *Bentboy*, producers should feel free to use Indigenous traditions, language, and shelters that reflect the area where the performances will be taking place. In the script, the village is created with tipis, and the song is sung in Anishinaabemowin, but these details can be changed to align with other First Nations.

In the YPT production, the staging featured long panels of cloth stretching from floor to ceiling, and a ramp that images could be projected onto. Other set pieces were moved on and offstage as needed. Projections included forest scenes, maps, a pathway, people shaking hands, etc. The main consideration is to create a flexible set that can represent many different locations, and which can transform quickly and easily.

Village Life

The shadow of a woman, a grand woman, powerful, graceful and older, appears behind a scrim. This is EAGLESEYE, the elder. Her shadow passes from one side of the stage to the other with ease, and she then steps out from behind the scrim to speak directly to the audience.

EAGLESEYE: Each pathway is created by the single steps of many who go before. We, as the people, must be sure of the footsteps we take in order to make the pathway safe for our children to follow. This journey takes place before the coming of the European; a time of great peace. When our trade routes covered most of Turtle Island, disagreements were settled by games, and promises given were promises kept. This may seem to be a perfect world, but a perfect world comes from hard work and much learning, and each lesson a journey.

EAGLESEYE looks worriedly to the sky. She raises her hands to the sky and shadows of people start to create the world that the old woman lives in.

A woman makes her way across the stage, basket in hand, full of grains and plants; she goes over to a slight ledge in the stones leading up the path and takes her place. One by one, other VILLAGERS enter and find their places. Some set up homes. Each time one villager passes another, they acknowledge each other.

Atop the hillside, children run and play. We hear and catch sight of one in particular, HUMMINGBIRD. This handsome, healthy, young man chases the satchel used in the game they are playing. He is about to run back when he notices EAGLESEYE sitting on the rock.

HUMMINGBIRD: Grandmother, this is truly the most beautiful day I have known.

EAGLESEYE laughs.

EAGLESEYE: My grandson, every day is a gift. None more beautiful than any other. Is it not the days of rain that quench Mother Earth's tongue so she will have the energy to feed us? Is it not the snowy winters that let the trees sleep from the long endless work they do to shelter and keep us in the clean air?

HUMMINGBIRD: Truly, Grandmother! It is also the cold days I sit and learn from you, and hear the stories of times before, that are a gift.

EAGLESEYE: Yes, every day has its purpose as does each of us, and right now your purpose is to continue your game.

Go. We will speak later.

HUMMINGBIRD runs off and joins the game, and once again we hear the laughter and screams of joy from the children.

EAGLESEYE: *(To the audience.)* It is my role now to teach not only with what I say, but with my actions too—the way I live and also the way I have lived in the past. Hummingbird has all of his days in front of him but that also means all of his lessons are in front of him too. *(She laughs.)*

Two young people, DEERCHILD and GREYFOWL, enter carrying a large deer on a branch. They are proud of the hunt.

DEERCHILD: Eagleseye, the valley is filled with deer, enough to feed our families till the mountains are flattened by the rain.

GREYFOWL: Deerchild and I were thinking that if we were to bring back a few more deer we could feast, and all in the village would be stuffed and happy.

EAGLESEYE: Just because the Creator makes it so plentiful does not mean we should take it. We have enough to feed all. There is no need for us to be stuffed, just happy. How would you feel if, like the deer, you were given so little concern? If you were merely a number?

DEERCHILD: But Eagleseye, they are merely deer...

EAGLESEYE: ...and we are merely human...

GREYFOWL: Forgive our greed, Eagleseye.

DEERCHILD: *(Whispering to GREYFOWL.)* Why must we care about the deer...

The two walk off to continue their work as EAGLESEYE listens to the children. Suddenly the laughter ends, and jeers replace it. BENTBOY hobbles away from where they are playing. He is a small boy who is sickly looking. A curvature of the spine has left him hunched over and his muscles ache from trying to keep this unbalanced load upright. You can clearly see on his face the disappointment of not keeping up with the other kids and he looks back, wishing they would call him back. He wanders down the hill, barely able to stay on his feet on the uneven path that leads him down to the village. He is so sad he doesn't even notice EAGLESEYE watching him.

EAGLESEYE: Hello, Bentboy. Why are you so down?

BENTBOY: Only because of the curve in my spine.

BENTBOY laughs at his own joke while EAGLESEYE does not.

BENTBOY: Just a joke, Eagleseye. I'm not down. Just watching my step to make sure nothing trips up these lazy feet of mine.

BENTBOY gives her a smile.

EAGLESEYE: Why are you not up with the other children playing?

BENTBOY: I was, but they...they...well, I was just too slow for them and I was keeping the game from being fun.

EAGLESEYE: Is that what they told you?

BENTBOY: No, they didn't say that. I just noticed is all, and well, it was not fun anymore. Please, Eagleseye, don't mention it to them. I want it to be our secret.

EAGLESEYE: Fine, Bentboy, I'll say nothing.

BENTBOY: Besides, there is much to do here in the village.

> *BENTBOY starts to walk away as EAGLESEYE watches. He stops and awkwardly turns to EAGLESEYE.*

BENTBOY: Eagleseye, have you ever wished you were someone else?

EAGLESEYE: No...

> *BENTBOY realizes he might have opened up a can of worms he does not want opened and tries to cover it up.*

BENTBOY: *(Quickly.)* Yeah, me neither.

> *BENTBOY exits, leaving EAGLESEYE to contemplate. As he does, her young grandson returns to the village.*

> *HUMMINGBIRD rolls a buckskin ball toward the tipi,[1] then goes over to the water bucket and takes a drink. EAGLESEYE looks at her grandson and asks:*

EAGLESEYE: Well, Grandson, how was the game today?

HUMMINGBIRD: Good, Grandmother.

EAGLESEYE: Did you have fun?

HUMMINGBIRD: I did.

EAGLESEYE: And the others?

---

[1] Or other type of traditional Indigenous shelter.

HUMMINGBIRD: They all had fun, Grandmother, even the young ones. They have learned the rules real well. Beaverstooth is getting so good.

EAGLESEYE: As good as you?

HUMMINGBIRD: No way, Grandmother, I am the best. Nobody even comes close.

EAGLESEYE: What about Bentboy? How good is he?

HUMMINGBIRD: Bentboy? He's not good at all, Grandmother. I am not trying to be mean or anything, but he doesn't even know the rules. No matter how much I try to teach him he plays...well, different. Wrong. There is one way to play this game and he doesn't know how to play it.

> *HUMMINGBIRD runs off, leaving EAGLESEYE to think before she too walks off in the same direction. From out of one of the tipis comes BENTBOY, who looks off after them. He walks to the pathway, sits down and thinks, resting his head with his eyes closed.*

> *The world around him changes. When he opens his eyes, he stands up, looks around and slowly straightens his spine. He suddenly dances around with the freedom to move, almost taking flight, until he is winded and ends up back at the place he started.*

> *His eyes close and his world returns to normal. He opens his eyes once again, stands up and tries to straighten up, getting only to his regular bent shape, then tries to fly again only to find he can't.*

Feast of Fear

> *Out of the homes come the VILLAGERS,
> and they begin getting ready for a large
> feast. There is the hustle and bustle of
> life all around, each person doing exactly
> what they should and singing a beautiful
> Anishinaabe song.*

ALL:
> *(In Anishinaabemowin:[2])*
> The journey of life is a long road
> This road holds twists and turns
> But with love and understanding
> And family to support
> The journey is a good one
> The good life

> *The preparing of the meal is like a dance,
> with people swaying and dodging when
> necessary, everybody working together…
> until BENTBOY enters. The first few
> people are lucky enough to avoid the boy
> but soon one bumps into him, which
> affects a second, and so on, until the
> whole dance ends in a tangled pile of
> villagers.*

> *BENTBOY reaches to the ground and
> picks up some spilled food and wanders
> back into the tipi as the villagers all voice
> their displeasure with him to each other
> and to EAGLESEYE.*

---

[2] Or other Indigenous language.

HUMMINGBIRD: You see, Grandmother?

ANONAMOUSE: Something must be done. We can't go on like this.

GREYFOWL: He has ruined the song!

HUMMINGBIRD: Grandmother, you have always told me that everyone has their place, their role. What is Bentboy's role other than being underfoot and causing messes?

EAGLESEYE: His role is...um...his place is...

HUMMINGBIRD: You don't even know, do you? Grandmother?

                  EAGLESEYE looks down at her young grandson and realizes nothing she could say can convince HUMMINGBIRD or the other villagers of BENTBOY's worth.

HUMMINGBIRD: He cannot hunt to bring in food. He can't carry much as his back will break...I don't mean to be rude, Grandmother, but I must be honest—if everyone here doesn't carry some of their weight, then should they sit at the feast?

                  HUMMINGBIRD walks away, leaving EAGLESEYE speechless. EAGLESEYE looks at her grandson as he helps clean the mess without saying a word.

The Journey Starts

Slowly the screens change, the once-blue sky is cloudy and darker. As the clouds start to surround EAGLESEYE, she raises her hand and pushes them away, and yet they still seem to envelop her.

EAGLESEYE: Now comes a dark time in the lives of our people.

The VILLAGERS collect themselves as they finish cleaning up and try to take their places at the feast.

EAGLESEYE: People, we are in grave danger. There is an enemy that will conquer the village soon and if it is not stopped, we will not survive.

Many years ago, my grandfather buried something that will help us. He buried it a long way away. Somebody must go and bring this box back here. There is only one among you who has the ability to do this. This young man not only has the strength to make this journey but the intelligence.

But know this—there are great dangers on this trip. This young man will be going through places we have not been in a long time and places we might not ever go back to.

HUMMINGBIRD stands.

HUMMINGBIRD: I will go, Grandmother, and I am honoured.

EAGLESEYE: Thank you, Hummingbird, but I am not sending you. I am sending Bentboy.

GREYFOWL: Bentboy!?!?!

DEERCHILD: He cannot do this.

HUMMINGBIRD: I can do it, Grandmother.

GREYFOWL: Yes, Hummingbird is strong. Send him!

DEERCHILD: If we are in danger let *us* choose who saves us!

HUMMINGBIRD: He is slow and weak and...well...broken. I'm not being mean, Grandmother. He is not fast of feet; he is under them.

EAGLESEYE: I think he should go and therefore he will go.

BENTBOY: Eagleseye...perhaps they are right.

EAGLESEYE: Bentboy, have you lost your faith in me?

BENTBOY: No...

EAGLESEYE: Good, because I have not lost faith in you. Now go get what you need. You have a long journey ahead of you.

> *BENTBOY goes to his tipi. The table and feast are slowly taken away. The mood of the village has changed. There is fear and sadness.*

DEERCHILD: *(To HUMMINGBIRD.)* Say something.

GREYFOWL:	*(To HUMMINGBIRD.)* Everyone agrees you should be the one to go.
HUMMINGBIRD:	Grandmother, must Bentboy go? I know I can—
EAGLESEYE:	He will go.

HUMMINGBIRD understands and knows the wise woman will not change her mind. It's at this time that a village lady pushes BENTBOY out of the tipi.

EAGLESEYE:	Ahhh, Bentboy. Are you ready for your journey?

The lady who pushed BENTBOY out hands him a pack. BENTBOY puts it on his back.

BENTBOY:	Yes, Eagleseye, I am honoured you chose me.
HUMMINGBIRD:	You're not scared?
BENTBOY:	Oh yes! Very, but it is a journey that must be taken.
EAGLESEYE:	Time to go. On this scroll is the route you must take. *(She hands BENTBOY a scroll).* Take care.

The VILLAGERS wave sadly as they realize that all hope of survival is resting on BENTBOY's shoulders.

It's Just a Creek

> *BENTBOY walks along, talking to himself. Large stones can be seen leading across the creek, almost like a pathway. The water is hardly a trickle.*

BENTBOY: That box could have anything in it. Maybe a weapon, like a spear or an arrow made of stone that would hold off any enemy. It could be a seed for a new food that could keep us fed if we are running out.

> *He starts to cross the creek. He makes the first rock and regains his balance then jumps to the second, almost falling, but again taking the time to regain his footing. Just before he takes his next jump, he slips and falls into the creek. He is completely wet from head to foot.*

BENTBOY: Well, I have fallen into the creek. What a silly thing for me to do. Oh no, look! I have gotten the map wet. It is completely gone. I have no clue where to go. Maybe I should return to the village… No. Have faith in yourself, Bentboy. You will find the box.

> *HUMMINGBIRD comes running in to find BENTBOY sitting in the creek. He is out of breath as he has been running.*

HUMMINGBIRD:	There you are, Bentboy. I knew you wouldn't get too far. Why are you sitting in the creek?
BENTBOY:	I fell.
HUMMINGBIRD:	In that little water?

HUMMINGBIRD leaps from rock to rock showing off his talents.

BENTBOY:	Hummingbird. What are you doing here? ...Your grandmother sent you?
HUMMINGBIRD:	She knows nothing. She thinks you can do this but nobody else does. I am here to help you
BENTBOY:	I don't need help.
HUMMINGBIRD:	You can't tie your own moccasins. How can you get the box that will save the whole village?
BENTBOY:	I can. I will. Eagleseye asked me to do it, I won't let her down.
HUMMINGBIRD:	Just give me the scroll and I will find the treasure. Wait here and I will bring it back. Then you can stay safe and I can save the village.
BENTBOY:	No.
HUMMINGBIRD:	Bentboy, there are many dangers out there. Things you don't understand. Things that can hurt you or worse. You nearly drowned in this much water. *(Holding two fingers up.)*
BENTBOY:	Well, I won't give you the map. You don't know where to go without the map.

HUMMINGBIRD: You may not give me the map, but you can't stop me from following.

BENTBOY: Fine... we are going ...umm...

                BENTBOY looks at the blank map and pretends to read it. Turns it a number of ways then points, pretending to read the map.

BENTBOY: That way.

                HUMMINGBIRD starts to walk off.

HUMMINGBIRD: Dry yourself off and come on. It's a long journey.

                He points to the ground in front of him.

HUMMINGBIRD: Let me know if you need a hand getting over this pebble!

                HUMMINGBIRD walks off laughing as BENTBOY collects himself and gets up ready to march on.

BENTBOY: *(To himself.)* ...But I don't want your help...

                He gets up and tries to catch up to HUMMINGBIRD.

A Thousand Steps and the Stone People

HUMMINGBIRD takes a seat at the bottom of a great rocky hill. He gets up and looks back to where he came from and sits back down, looks to the sun and then back to where he came from. He pulls out a cloth, unwraps it and eats a little food from it, wraps it back up and puts it away.

He rests back and waits. BENTBOY comes along singing a traditional song very poorly. He is tired but happy.

BENTBOY: Did you see that fox? They were hiding down the path way back there. He followed us for a long way, but I wasn't scared. I was fascinated. I kept looking back and the fox would hide behind a tree and then stick their nose out and watch then duck behind and then just walk along the tree line watching us. Hey, do you think they are telling their friends about us just like I am telling you? That is something. I mean not talking like us but in fox language, or maybe Anishinaabemowin. I don't know, maybe the animals do talk like us. If they do that would be something, because then I would want to catch a live one and ask him what it would be like to be a fox, but he may not know what to say. I mean, if the fox asked me what it is like to be a boy,

I wouldn't know what to tell him. I'd just say, "Hey, this is all I know, so Mr. Fox, if you need some—"

HUMMINGBIRD: That fox was following you because he was trying to figure out what strange creature was making so much noise. You never mind about that fox. Foxes are small, but they are dangerous. They will bite you.

BENTBOY is silenced.

HUMMINGBIRD: Now if you don't mind, we have a long way to go. No more watching the trees grow or the creek fill with fish—just eyes on the path. There is only one way to get there and if we stay focused, we'll get there sooner. This way? *(Pointing up the hill.)*

BENTBOY pulls out the map and makes believe he is reading it. He nods to HUMMINGBIRD, who gets up and starts up the hill, leaving BENTBOY alone.

BENTBOY: But then, how will we learn?

HUMMINGBIRD: Bentboy, if we don't keep moving we will never get done. Is that what you want? I want to get back home as soon as possible.

BENTBOY: Then go back home. You were not chosen for this journey. This is my journey. I was chosen.

HUMMINGBIRD: I am here to help you. You and I know you can't do this alone. Just do what I do, and you'll be fine.

HUMMINGBIRD starts up the hill but is pushed down by a ROCK. He rolls down to the feet of BENTBOY.

BENTBOY: What happened?

HUMMINGBIRD: I was pushed down.

BENTBOY: Really...but there is nobody there.

HUMMINGBIRD: Something pushed me.

BENTBOY: Maybe you tripped.

HUMMINGBIRD: I never trip.

HUMMINGBIRD angrily marches up the hill while BENTBOY looks around. HUMMINGBIRD again is pushed down.

HUMMINGBIRD: It happened again.

BENTBOY: You fell?

HUMMINGBIRD: NO! I WAS PUSHED!

HUMMINGBIRD and BENTBOY look to the hillside. There is no movement and no sign of anyone who could have pushed HUMMINGBIRD.

BENTBOY: That rock pushed you down the hill.

HUMMINGBIRD: The hills don't want us to get the treasure.

BENTBOY: But why?

HUMMINGBIRD: Grandmother told me. She said that the hills don't want man to succeed. The hills think that man has a heavy foot and will pound the hills flat.

BENTBOY: Then we have to—

HUMMINGBIRD: You must be quiet and do not move. I will fight the rocks myself.

BENTBOY: But we could get by them if we—

HUMMINGBIRD: Look, if anything happens to you I have to go back and tell the village. Then they will know I followed. You must do as I tell you if you want to be unharmed. Now stay still. The hills can't see—they only know you are there by feeling your footsteps.

> *BENTBOY does not move. HUMMING-BIRD starts up the hill with anger, feet pounding and the walking stick he carries swinging. The ROCKS get up from where they lay and move toward the young man. He readies himself for battle. They battle for a while as BENTBOY watches. HUMMINGBIRD has a difficult time fighting the ROCKS and the battle goes back and forth. BENTBOY gets up and calls to Hummingbird.*

BENTBOY: Do you want my help?

> *The ROCKS all change their focus as BENTBOY walks toward the fight.*

HUMMINGBIRD: Don't move! They know where you are!

> *BENTBOY freezes. The ROCKS switch focus back to HUMMINGBIRD. The fight continues while BENTBOY has an idea. He fashions a pair of moccasins from some bulrushes and slips them onto his feet.*

He then quietly tiptoes toward the path up the mountain. He stops to see if they have noticed him and continues when he sees they have not. The fight goes on around him without a ROCK or HUMMINGBIRD noticing him.

Reaching the top, he sits and waits as HUMMINGBIRD slowly fights off every ROCK on his way to the top. When HUMMINGBIRD gets to the summit, he turns to tell BENTBOY to come up.

HUMMINGBIRD: *(Looking down.)* Okay, quick, get up here and don't hold me up.

BENTBOY: I am here.

HUMMINGBIRD is startled to find BENTBOY at the top of the hill.

HUMMINGBIRD: How did...?

BENTBOY: I just made it so my—

HUMMINGBIRD: Never mind. It is a good thing I fought off the rocks. Had you been on this trip alone you would be buried by the hill by now.

BENTBOY: Thank you, Hummingbird.

HUMMINGBIRD: We should keep going. We have a long way to go with little time.

BENTBOY wanders off again, singing off key. HUMMINGBIRD, catching his breath, notices the bulrush shoes BENTBOY has left behind, then catches up to BENTBOY.

When the Wind Blows

The two boys enter the forest. The sky builds up clouds and the leaves begin to shake with the wind. A leaf falls off a branch and floats on the wind. The two boys enter, fighting against the wind, while BENTBOY chatters away.

BENTBOY: I feel like I will be blown away with this wind. It is so strong. Not as strong as you though, huh? You just keep on going, I see that. There is no stopping you. I see you are determined to keep going. Are you getting cold? The wind feels much colder to me...

More leaves are being pulled off the branches and thrown around, and with the cold come snowflakes. The wind builds up more and more.

BENTBOY: Did you see that? Here comes the snow. Will we stop for the snow? I think we should stop.

BENTBOY slips and catches himself.

BENTBOY: Ouch, I just slipped. Hummingbird, I slipped. This is not good.

HUMMINGBIRD: Look, Bentboy, you were very lucky to get past the rocks. Our village is in danger and we have to return before there is nothing left. The slower we are, the more chance we will go home to nothing.

BENTBOY:	There is no way we can get through. Storms like this are dangerous.
HUMMINGBIRD:	Storms like this might be dangerous for people like you but not for me. I am strong. You are...we have to go on.
BENTBOY:	I can't, Hummingbird.
HUMMINGBIRD:	Then you stay here. I'll come back for you.
BENTBOY:	No.
HUMMINGBIRD:	Yes, give me the scroll.
BENTBOY:	This is my journey, Hummingbird.
HUMMINGBIRD:	You can't keep up with me and we are running out of time!

BENTBOY lowers his head, knowing that is true.

HUMMINGBIRD:	If you catch up, I'll give you back the scroll and you can lead.
BENTBOY:	I will catch up when the storm is over.
HUMMINGBIRD:	You won't. I will be too far ahead of you and you are not as fast as I am.
BENTBOY:	Okay, but you have to promise me you won't open the scroll...until you really need it....I...I don't want it to get ruined in this storm. I will catch up to you before you need it! promise?
HUMMINGBIRD:	I promise.
BENTBOY:	I will catch up.
HUMMINGBIRD:	You can try, Bentboy.
BENTBOY:	I will.

As BENTBOY goes to work building a small lean-to on the side of a tree and enters to be sheltered and warm, HUMMINGBIRD starts his walk into the wind, but stops. Looks back at the lean-to to make sure BENTBOY is not looking and then begins to unroll the scroll. BENTBOY hides within as HUMMINGBIRD continues on his journey.

The NORTH WIND appears in the form of a person with spikes extending five feet out from his body. NORTH WIND smiles and steals the scroll from HUMMINGBIRD. NORTH WIND floats it teasingly away from HUMMINGBIRD, who struggles to get it back. They dance/fight with each other—HUMMINGBIRD with pure struggle and the NORTH WIND with pure enjoyment. This goes on until HUMMINGBIRD, too tired to fight anymore, falls to the floor.

The stage is bathed in daylight one more time, and from the shelter emerges BENTBOY. He gets himself ready, bending and stretching like he has just been asleep for a million years. He turns and runs right into HUMMINGBIRD passed out on the floor, not two feet from the spot his journey began. BENTBOY says nothing at first then leans down beside HUMMINGBIRD.

BENTBOY: What are you listening for now?

HUMMINGBIRD looks up with both tired and angered eyes.

BENTBOY: I caught up!

BENTBOY reaches down and snatches the scroll back.

HUMMINGBIRD: Of course you did. I had to wait for you.

BENTBOY: I knew it. You couldn't go on without me. Now follow me.

HUMMINGBIRD: I am right behind you.

The two go off together with BENTBOY leading, looking around at all that he passes, as HUMMINGBIRD lags behind.

I Need a Rest

From around some trees we hear the sound of BENTBOY talking.

BENTBOY:

...and the fox was there but I don't think they saw me until I said hello. That's how I got that close to it; almost close enough to touch it. I mean that close! And they just looked up and disappeared. I have never seen that before. Have you ever seen that before? Not a fox, but something disappear? I don't mean it was fast, it was just gone, disappeared. Do you think it was a spirit like a guide following? Ohhhh, could it be your grandmother? Can she shape-shift?

BENTBOY emerges from behind a tree, stops and looks around. HUMMINGBIRD is not there.

BENTBOY:

Hummingbird? Hummingbird? Where are you?

BENTBOY goes back behind the trees and looks for HUMMINGBIRD, and then they both come out. HUMMINGBIRD is very tired.

BENTBOY:

Wow, you were way back there. A long way back. I have never seen you tired. I only get to see your back and from the back you never look tired but from the front you look very tired; really, really tired, more tired than I have ever seen.

HUMMINGBIRD: Please, Bentboy, stop talking. I am too tired. We should settle for the night and set up camp here.

BENTBOY: Remember, Hummingbird, I am leading... and I think we should camp for the night.

The boys set up camp. HUMMINGBIRD lights a fire and the two settle in for the night as it gets dark. The fire flickers as the two boys crawl into their bedrolls.

BENTBOY: You must be tired from fighting all day.

Silence.

HUMMINGBIRD: I'm not. I didn't fight.

Silence.

BENTBOY: Why did you fight them all?

HUMMINGBIRD turns over in the bedroll and faces BENTBOY.

HUMMINGBIRD: Because, Bentboy. Because they were trying to hurt us. I had to.

Silence.

BENTBOY: Ohh...

Silence as HUMMINGBIRD rolls back over, facing away from BENTBOY.

BENTBOY: How did you know so fast?

HUMMINGBIRD rolls back over to face BENTBOY.

HUMMINGBIRD: I could tell by the look on their faces, Bentboy. They looked mean.

BENTBOY: Ohhh, I had not noticed that. Because of my spine it's usually the last thing I get to see.

> *BENTBOY rolls over, leaving HUMMINGBIRD thinking.*

HUMMINGBIRD: What do you mean?

BENTBOY: Well, because of my spine being as curved as the creek, I don't get to see faces. I have to look at the feet then work my way up to the knees and then hips and the—

HUMMINGBIRD: I get it. By the time you get to the face you will have been eaten.

> *BENTBOY thinks about this for a moment.*

BENTBOY: Strange I haven't been eaten yet.

HUMMINGBIRD: Well, you're lucky.

> *BENTBOY is surprised and laughs a full belly laugh.*

HUMMINGBIRD: What?

BENTBOY: Nobody has ever said I was lucky before.

HUMMINGBIRD: Well...

BENTBOY: Sometimes I don't feel so lucky.

HUMMINGBIRD: That's not what I meant.

BENTBOY: I guess I am lucky, because...you know, I start at the feet and work my way to the face and by the time I'm there I can almost always see why the face is mad. Could be that it is a hurt knee or a heavy weight on the shoulders. Even the smallest toe can make it too uncomfortable for a giant to walk. Sometimes I notice these things. Nothing is ever born angry.

With that, BENTBOY turns over in his bedroll and drifts off to sleep. HUMMINGBIRD is left looking at the lump in the bedroll, thinking about what BENTBOY has said.

Lights fade out.

The Morning Hug

The next morning. The boys are asleep. All around them are CLINGING VINES that have wrapped the boys up. The boys wake to find themselves unable to move. HUMMINGBIRD starts to fight again while BENTBOY waits. It's not long before HUMMINGBIRD notices BENTBOY with no fight, and he thinks about what he had said the night before. He stops his struggle.

As the light from the sun gets bigger and brighter, the VINES that have wrapped themselves around the boys start to back away, releasing the boys.

BENTBOY: I thought you would fight but you didn't.

HUMMINGBIRD: I started to…then I remembered what you said last night about noticing things. How did you know the plants would let us go?

BENTBOY: I could feel it when I woke up. The vine wasn't squeezing, it was just hugging. Then I was thinking, why does anyone hug?

HUMMINGBIRD shrugs his shoulders.

BENTBOY: Love!

HUMMINGBIRD: Right, love! Of course.

BENTBOY: But plants don't need love; they need warmth.

HUMMINGBIRD: Of course.

BENTBOY: So I waited and I thought that when the sun came out there would be enough warmth that the plant would relax and then the plant might be thankful for the warmth.

HUMMINGBIRD: What do you mean?

BENTBOY reaches into his pouch and the tops of his moccasins and pulls out fresh berries that the plant has left behind. HUMMINGBIRD does the same. They both eat while they get ready to leave, talking and laughing the whole time.

Sucked Down

The boys go deeper into the woods. The sky is darker now and it is starting to rain. The ground is an earth path leading up to a single bare tree in the middle of the stage with the old branches reaching in all different directions. The tree looks as old as the ground that holds it. The boys are talking to each other for the first time on this journey and are getting their fill of the berries left in their pockets.

HUMMINGBIRD: ...but I told you when we were playing you can't use your hands on the skin. It's part of the rules.

BENTBOY: I heard you but it's hard for me to kick anything because I am always on one side. If I lift my foot I would fall over.

The TREE opens its eyes.

HUMMINGBIRD: Are you getting tired? We could rest for a bit.

BENTBOY: Are you sure? I could try to go on.

HUMMINGBIRD: No, no, you sit down, relax for a bit. We have time. Besides, it's starting to rain. We can use this old tree for shelter. Seems the only thing this old tree is good for is to hide under. Like you, Bentboy, his spine is crooked and if you leaned on it too hard it would fall over, just like you.

Maybe we could pull your legs and your arms to straighten your back.

BENTBOY: We could try but I don't think it would do much good.

HUMMINGBIRD: Then you can be like me.

BENTBOY: Ummmm...I like you, Hummingbird, but I also like me. I don't want to change.

HUMMINGBIRD: But don't you want to be like everyone else? I mean, your life would be easier. Everyone wants to be part of something, Bentboy.

BENTBOY: Hummingbird, look. This tree is different from any other tree you have seen on our journey.

HUMMINGBIRD: Yes.

BENTBOY: And yet this tree is part of the forest.

HUMMINGBIRD: But if your spine was straight you could hunt and play and carry wood. You could be part of the village instead of, well, on the outside.

BENTBOY, wanting to move on from the conversation, pulls the map out.

BENTBOY: Well, let's go. That way.

BENTBOY points in the direction they came from.

HUMMINGBIRD: But that's the way we came.

BENTBOY: Did we?

HUMMINGBIRD: Let me look at the map.

> *He goes to grab it but BENTBOY tries to stop him.*

HUMMINGBIRD: Come on.

BENTBOY: No, I don't think...

HUMMINGBIRD: You can keep it. I just want to look.

BENTBOY: No, it's—

> *HUMMINGBIRD grabs the map and looks at it and then flips it over to show the other side. He sees nothing.*

HUMMINGBIRD: Where is the map?

BENTBOY: You have it.

HUMMINGBIRD: There is nothing here.

BENTBOY: *(Sadly.)* I know. It got washed away in the creek.

HUMMINGBIRD: Way back there!!! You knew it WAY BACK THERE!!! We are lost, in the middle of nowhere. How could you, Bentboy? Not only are you in the way back in the village, but out here you cause even more trouble!!! We may never get home and even if we do, we won't have the treasure!!! You had to do one thing; follow the map and bring the treasure home. You didn't!! Did you?

> *HUMMINGBIRD walks around yelling, not able to look at BENTBOY.*

HUMMINGBIRD: I told my grandmother this was a huge mistake!! That you couldn't do it!! That you couldn't do anything!! People don't want you around!! They wish you would just disappear!!!!!!

As this conversation goes on, the rain softens the ground around the roots of the tree and BENTBOY sinks into the ground. We watch the ground suck BENTBOY under. HUMMINGBIRD doesn't notice.

HUMMINGBIRD comes around the tree only to find BENTBOY missing.

HUMMINGBIRD: Bentboy? Bentboy?! Where are you?

HUMMINGBIRD looks all over for BENTBOY, running around the tree and searching for any clue of his whereabouts. Only after searching all over does he notice one of BENTBOY's moccasins by the root and the remnants of a hole left by the body of BENTBOY. He tries to dig but the roots of the TREE stop him. He runs off, looking for something to help him get to BENTBOY.

Outside the Tree

> *HUMMINGBIRD is busy trying to dig BENTBOY out from the hole with a shell, but the roots are as strong as concrete.*

TREE: Why do you dig at my roots?

HUMMINGBIRD: Under them holds Bentboy! You must let him go.

TREE: Must I?

HUMMINGBIRD: Yes. I promised Bentboy I would take care of him and my word is important.

TREE: Is it?

HUMMINGBIRD: Yes! My words mean everything to me.

TREE: You know your words fill the air and are passed on the wind. I have heard your words.

HUMMINGBIRD: Then you know I speak the truth.

TREE: Yes, I do. You spoke of Bentboy's uselessness. You said "Those who don't carry their weight shouldn't sit at the table." Wasn't it you who told your grandmother that Bentboy "couldn't do this journey" and that Bentboy "couldn't do anything"?

HUMMINGBIRD: ...I was angry.

TREE: Hurtful words spoken in anger don't hurt any less than hurtful words spoken any other way.

                  HUMMINGBIRD attacks the roots of the TREE.

TREE: Why do you continue to dig at my roots?

HUMMINGBIRD: I must save Bentboy!

TREE: Why do you care what happens to Bentboy? Didn't you want him gone? Your wish is granted. Go.

HUMMINGBIRD: I won't.

                  Still digging.

TREE: You do see that that won't work? My roots are strong. They have to be to hold up my heavy, bent body.

HUMMINGBIRD: Then I will dig and dig and dig.

TREE: Even though you know it won't work. Why?

HUMMINGBIRD: Because it is how it is done.

TREE: Won't you get tired?

HUMMINGBIRD: My arms are strong!

TREE: Ahhh, but I have strong roots. I have seen a lot of strong trees fall around me. Even the smallest breeze can snap a thick branch. I am very old. I have learned at times to let the water move by my roots rather than to try and stop the water because if you don't bend then you break.

                  HUMMINGBIRD wears himself out and collapses at the base of the TREE.

TREE:	Someday you will make a great leader. Until that day you must be a better student and listen more.
HUMMINGBIRD:	It doesn't really matter, we'll never make it back in time. We are lost.
TREE:	Sometimes lost is right where you need to be.
HUMMINGBIRD:	Bentboy would know what to do!
TREE:	Would he?
HUMMINGBIRD:	Yes. He would look at things in a different way.
TREE:	Then look differently.

HUMMINGBIRD looks to the TREE and puts down the hard shell. He looks closely at the roots and then he discovers the hole that BENTBOY vanished into. He reaches in and pulls out a large cedar chest.

HUMMINGBIRD:	The box! This is what Grandmother was talking about.
TREE:	You have the box! You can save the village. You can be the hero.
HUMMINGBIRD:	But what about Bentboy?
TREE:	Why do you need him? He will only slow you down.

HUMMINGBIRD looks at the box but quickly throws it away and returns to the task at hand. He reaches back into the hole.

HUMMINGBIRD:	Bentboy! Take my hand. I can pull you up?!!
BENTBOY:	.....No....
HUMMINGBIRD:	No?
BENTBOY:	I can't do anything. Nobody wants me around. I should just disappear.
HUMMINGBIRD:	That's not true, Bentboy. We need you...I need you. Every forest needs trees and every tree is special.
	You have found the box, Bentboy.
BENTBOY:	Yes, but I wouldn't have gotten it out without you.
HUMMINGBIRD:	Yes, but I can't get home without you... Bentboy, I need you.
	There is a moment of silence.We then see BENTBOY's hand reach out from under the tree. HUMMINGBIRD takes it and pulls BENTBOY to the surface.
BENTBOY:	No, you don't. You would have found it. You're so strong and smart. You would have found it.
HUMMINGBIRD:	No, Bentboy, I don't think I would have. I would have spent my whole time fighting.
BENTBOY:	You could have left me here after I gave you the box.
HUMMINGBIRD:	This old tree wanted me to, but I wouldn't.
BENTBOY:	Ha, that is funny!! An old tree talking to you!

HUMMINGBIRD: It did!

BENTBOY: We need to go and get this box back to Eagleseye before it's too late!

> *HUMMINGBIRD looks at the tree, hoping for the tree to talk but it doesn't.*

HUMMINGBIRD: Say something, tree!

BENTBOY: Come, let's go!

> *HUMMINGBIRD gives up and picks up the box and walks off leaving BENTBOY alone onstage.*

BENTBOY: Thank you, tree.

> *He touches the trunk of the TREE and walks away.*

TREE: …You're welcome.

The River

> *The boys walk for a while until they finally come to the river. It is deep and wide.*

HUMMINGBIRD: The water is too deep.

BENTBOY: I know. The creek has gotten deeper from all the rain.

HUMMINGBIRD: So what should we do?

BENTBOY: You are asking me?

HUMMINGBIRD: Of course I am. You have gotten us this far, right?

> *BENTBOY is shocked and moved by this but soon regains himself.*

BENTBOY: We should make a boat.

> *The boys get to work and soon build a boat. They get in and start to cross the river. The river swirls and dances around them, turning the boat in all different directions.*
>
> *BENTBOY, who is in the front and facing forward, is trying to hold on. HUMMINGBIRD is in the back. He has the paddle out of the water and is just watching the waves throw the boat around in a dance. The boat starts to crack and creak like it is being torn apart. BENTBOY looks back and sees that HUMMINGBIRD is not paddling.*

BENTBOY: What are you doing?!?

HUMMINGBIRD: I'm not fighting the river!

BENTBOY: I'm pretty sure this is a time you should be fighting.

HUMMINGBIRD: I'm not even supposed to be here.

BENTBOY: Yes, but you are, so start fighting!

> *HUMMINGBIRD gets to work paddling. The boat continues to be thrown around but HUMMINGBIRD and BENTBOY work together and bring the boat to solid ground on the other side of the river. They hug and yell back at the river.*

HUMMINGBIRD: We did it!

BENTBOY: Yes, and this time I didn't get wet...well, not that wet.

HUMMINGBIRD: No, we did it. All of it. I can see the smoke from the campfires in our village.

> *HUMMINGBIRD, excited, picks up the box and takes a step toward the village. He stops and looks back at BENTBOY, who is struggling to get up in his awkward manner. HUMMINGBIRD puts the box on the ground and waits for BENTBOY to get up.*

HUMMINGBIRD: Ummm, Bentboy, can you help me?

BENTBOY: You can carr— Sure.

HUMMINGBIRD: I wonder where that fox you saw is now.

BENTBOY: I don't know but he seemed like a nice fox. I bet he is just waiting for us by the big oak tree, right where we last saw him...

Home Again

The village is as it was before the boys left. EAGLESEYE enters and sits at her place and waits. A MAN runs in and shows her a load of fish then runs off to clean it. A WOMAN shoos DEERCHILD, who runs all the way up the cliffside and nearly bumps into BENTBOY and HUMMINGBIRD, who are entering, carrying the chest.

DEERCHILD: They're back! They are back!

All of the VILLAGERS run into the village square to welcome the boys home. They cheer and hug the boys as BENTBOY and HUMMINGBIRD work their way to EAGLESEYE. The two put the chest at the feet of EAGLESEYE. The VILLAGERS wait to hear her words.

EAGLESEYE: I am glad you have returned.

DEERCHILD: We were worried about you, Hummingbird.

GREYFOWL: Tell us of your trip.

HUMMINGBIRD: All of the elements you talk about are out there and they are strong.

DEERCHILD: And you beat them all down! Thank the Creator that Hummingbird went to save Bentboy.

VILLAGERS:	Yeah! Hooray! Amazing!
HUMMINGBIRD:	NO! No, I didn't. I would not have made it without Bentboy. He was the real strength behind this trip. I think he is a very important person and I think, too, he is my new friend.

The crowd is silenced for a second.

BENTBOY:	Hummingbird, you have always been my friend....
ANONAMOUSE:	More importantly, the treasure has been returned.
GREYFOWL:	Open it.
DEERCHILD:	Before the enemy invades.

EAGLESEYE lifts up the chest and the village goes quiet. She throws the chest into the fire. The VILLAGERS gasp and scream.

GREYFOWL:	No! The box. We are doomed!
DEERCHILD:	It was brought back too late!
ANONAMOUSE:	It's all Bentboy's fault!
GREYFOWL:	If he didn't slow Hummingbird down we would have been saved!
HUMMINGBIRD:	It's not true!!! I would have never found it without Bentboy. He knew how to get across the river. He snuck past the rocks with these *(Pulling the bulrush mocs from his bag.)* and knew when to fight and when not to. If I had listened and learned from him I might have been back here sooner.

BENTBOY: Why did you burn the box after we made that long journey to retrieve the treasure?

Again, the crowd goes quiet to hear the words of EAGLESEYE.

EAGLESEYE: It is simple, my boy. The treasure was not in the box but in the journey to get the box.

GREYFOWL: But what of the enemy?

ANONAMOUSE: How will we stop them?

BENTBOY: ...and who are they?

HUMMINGBIRD: They...are us. When we think we are more important than the animals, or the elements...or other humans, *(Looking at BENTBOY.)* we forget our place. When we don't know our place, we are lost.

The whole village breathes a sigh of relief and VILLAGERS resume their activities. Some are listening to BENTBOY as he tells the story of the journey. HUMMINGBIRD and EAGLESEYE watch with smiles on their faces.

You knew I was going to follow all along, didn't you, Grandmother?

EAGLESEYE: Oh?

HUMMINGBIRD: I didn't trust that Bentboy could do it. I thought that I needed to save him...

HUMMINGBIRD gets distracted by a pattern on the wall of one of the homes. He looks at it one way then twists his body in strange ways looking at the design then gets on his knees and twists again looking at the design. EAGLESEYE notices this and wonders.

EAGLESEYE: What are you doing, my boy?

HUMMINGBIRD: Bentboy taught me to look at things differently. I will never see the world in the same way again.

EAGLESEYE: You are so wise, Grandson.

HUMMINGBIRD: But not as wise as you, Grandmother.

EAGLESEYE: You will be. You know I, too, had to take the same journey as you, many years ago.

HUMMINGBIRD: Really?

EAGLESEYE: Really. Look, you see now peace has returned to the village and all will be good. Go and play, my grandson.

                  HUMMINGBIRD runs off to start a game with the children in the field. He stops and looks back at BENTBOY.

HUMMINGBIRD: You coming, Bentboy? We can try your new rules for the game.

                  As the boys run off, the song sung earlier starts to happen.

ALL: *(In Anishinaabemowin:[3])*
                  The journey of life is a long road
                  This road holds twists and turns
                  But with love and understanding
                  And family to support
                  The journey is a good one
                  The good life

                  The community again starts to set up for a feast as the song is sung softly in the background. EAGLESEYE speaks right to the audience.

---

[3] Or other Indigenous language.

EAGLESEYE: This journey is over. I think both learned so much. As did I. Sometimes we stumble on our journey and sometimes we fall, but we can get up and we can help others when they fall. Lucky for us, the song is back and true... the words are beautiful, are they not? No... oh, of course not many of you speak my language. Here, let me translate for you.

The song is sung by all again while EAGLESEYE speaks the words.

EAGLESEYE: The journey of life is a long one
This road holds many twists and turns
But with love and understanding
The riches of life we will earn

We all walk this pathway together
And the light and love we must share
The good life is a journey
But is lost if we forget to care

Lights fade.

The end.

Bentboy Study Guide

Bentboy Study Guide

This study guide was written by Lindy Kinoshameg with contributions from Molly Gardner. It was prepared for the Young People's Theatre production of Bentboy *and adapted slightly for publication in this book. It is reprinted here by permission of the authors and YPT.*

Thematic Overview

This story takes place in a time of "pre-contact," meaning before European settlers arrived on the shores of North America. This tale follows Hummingbird and Bentboy, two very different young boys who are finding their place within their community while being mentored by a wise elder known as Eagleseye. As each follows their own path, it becomes a journey that transforms them both. This play includes the themes of embracing the value of every person, redefining your community, and understanding your relationship to the natural world and each other. It is an adventure tale about finding strengths in our differences.

Synopsis

Hunched by his curved back, Bentboy is cast aside by his village until one day, when a dangerous threat to the community and their way of life is imminent, he is chosen by elder Eagleseye to embark on a quest to save the village. Along the way, Bentboy encounters an uninvited companion, Hummingbird. On this journey, the boys face off against nature and all of its wonders as they try to find a box which will save the village. Along the way they also discover each other's strengths and weaknesses, resulting in the boys learning to respect and trust one another and the wisdom in the world around them.

Curriculum Connections

The Arts – Drama, Dance,

Language

Health and Physical Education – Healthy Relationships, Social Emotional Learning

Social Studies – Heritage and Identity

Ancestral Teachings

Respect

Wisdom

Themes

Embracing the value of every person

Redefining community

Understanding our relationship to the natural world and each other

Glossary

TURTLE ISLAND:	Some First Nations refer to North America as Turtle Island.
SATCHEL:	A bag carried on the shoulder by a long strap and typically closed by a flap.
QUENCH:	To satisfy one's thirst.
CREATOR:	Another word for a spiritual entity, but could be a person or thing that brings something into existence.
"CAN OF WORMS":	A turn of phrase meaning to create a complicated situation in which doing something to correct a problem leads to many more problems.

ELDER: Someone who carries knowledge
                        and passes it on to the next
                        generation.

INTELLIGENCE: The ability to acquire and apply
                        knowledge and skills.

HONOUR: To regard with great respect.

SCROLL: A roll of paper or other material that
                        has writing or images on it.

MOCCASIN: A slipper or shoe made of soft
                        material such as leather.

ANISHINAABEMOWIN: A language used by specific First
                        Nations.

BULRUSH: A tall, rush-like water plant of
                        the sedge family, also known as a
                        cattail.

Units of Study

Through the discussion questions and activities in this study
guide, students will explore a "pre-contact" world and witness
the meaning of community for the Anishinaabe.

Students will create a space where multiple perspectives are
celebrated.

The activities are designed to let students explore the idea of
community and how differences and different abilities make
that community stronger.

Curriculum Expectations
Language

Identify the point of view presented in oral texts and ask
questions to identify missing or possible alternative points of
view.

Demonstrate an understanding of the information and ideas in oral texts by retelling the story or restating the information, including the main idea.

Identify, in conversation with the teacher and peers, what strategies they found most helpful before, during, and after listening and speaking and what steps they can take to improve their oral communication skills.

The Arts – Drama, Dance
Drama

∞ Engage in dramatic play and role-play, with a focus on exploring a variety of sources from diverse communities, times, and places.

∞ Express feelings and ideas about a drama experience or performance in a variety of ways, making personal connections to the characters and themes in the story.

∞ Express personal responses and make connections to characters, themes, and issues presented in their own and others' drama works.

Dance

∞ Use dance as a language to express feelings and ideas suggested by songs, stories, and poems, with a focus on the element of body, particularly body shapes.

∞ Use narrative form to create short dance pieces on a variety of themes.

Health and Physical Education: Healthy Relationships

∞ Apply skills that help build relationships, develop empathy, and communicate with others as they participate in learning experiences in health and physical education, in order to support healthy relationships, a sense of belonging, and respect for diversity.

Social Studies
Heritage and Identity: Our Changing Roles and Responsibilities

∞ Demonstrate an understanding that it is important to treat other people and the environment with respect.

∞ Describe the impact that people can have on each other in some different situations and some of the ways in which interactions between people can affect a person's sense of self.

Heritage and Identity: Early Societies to 1500 CE

∞ Formulate questions to guide investigations into ways of life and relationships with the environment in a few early societies, including at least one First Nation and one Inuit society, with an emphasis on aspects of the interrelationship between the environment and life in those societies.

People and Environments: The Local Community

∞ Create a plan that outlines some specific ways in which they can responsibly interact with the built and/ or natural environment in the local community and describe how their actions might enhance the features of the local environment.

Study Questions

∞ How do you interact with the natural world around you?

∞ How might other people, plants or animals view the world differently than you?

∞ Where do you see examples of "wisdom" within nature?

∞ What is a community? Name a community that you are part of.

∞ Is the destination or the journey more important to you? Why?

Exercise: This is not a pen...it's a....

Objective

This warm-up activity will offer students the opportunity to use their imaginations to transform objects, and then celebrate the way their peers may imagine differently than they do.

Preparation and Materials

Space to move.

Instructions

1. Ask students to choose one item in the class (something they can hold) and to imagine it as something else with an alternate use.

   (For example: "This is not a pen, it's a tele-communicator and I am a spy. This device allows me to receive orders from Headquarters, and report back that I have accomplished my mission, muahahaha!")

2. Allow each student to present their item to the rest of the class, and to describe it to the class. Encourage everyone to clap and cheer their fellow students on as they present their items.

Debriefing

∞ Was it interesting to see how your peers used their imaginations to come up with different ideas of what their object was? Why or why not?

∞ Was it easy or difficult to imagine what other people were sharing with you? Why?

∞ Is it important to consider other people's points of view? Why or why not? How can this skill be helpful in our day-to-day lives? Or helpful to our larger community?

Extensions

1. Choose one object for all students to use and see how many different ways the class can come up with different uses for the same object.

2. Set up the activity so that each student is trying to sell their item and needs to describe it to potential buyers.

Exercise: Name that object

Objective

This exercise offers students the opportunity to observe and practise different forms of communication, and to reflect on how all are valuable in different ways.

Preparation and Materials

Space to move.

Chart paper and markers.

Instructions

1. Ask for a pair of student volunteers, one participant and one who guesses, and ask them to stand at one end of the room with their backs turned from the rest of the class so that they cannot hear or see them. Have the other students seated as the audience.

2. Ask a volunteer from the audience to choose an object in the room that can be held safely (e.g., a book, a ruler, an eraser, etc.).

3. Call the participant over to the audience, let them see the object for ten seconds, and then assign them one of the following acts:

   ∞ Silently "act out" what the object is.

   ∞ Close your eyes, feel the object with your hands, then describe how it feels.

   ∞ Silently draw the object.

4. Next, call over the student who guesses but don't let them see the object. Have the participant use one of the communication strategies above and see if they can guess what the object is based on their partner's communication.

5. Repeat the exercise until all students have had the opportunity to participate.

Debriefing

∞ Which form of communication did you prefer? Was one form easier for you than another? Why?

∞ Is it important to try communicating in different ways? Why or why not?

∞ Do you think with practice people can get better at communicating in ways that they are not used to?

Extension

Have students bring in objects from home instead of using what is in the classroom.

Bentboy **Discussion Questions**

- ∞ How did Hummingbird treat Bentboy at the beginning of the play? How did that make Bentboy feel?

- ∞ Eagleseye said there was an "enemy that would conquer the village." After the journey, Hummingbird says "the enemy is us." Why does he think the village is its own enemy?

- ∞ Hummingbird always seemed to be in a rush to complete the quest. Was speed important for the journey the two boys went on? Why or why not?

- ∞ Hummingbird is physically strong, but when he uses all his might and power to overcome obstacles or nature, he is not always successful. Why is that?

- ∞ Would Bentboy have successfully completed his quest without Hummingbird? Why or why not? Would Hummingbird have been successful without Bentboy? Why or why not?

- ∞ The Tree used Hummingbird's words about Bentboy against him when he was trying to save him. Was that fair? Why or why not?

- ∞ At the end of the play, how have Bentboy and Hummingbird "saved" the village?

Exercise: Bentboy's Quest

Objective

A fun, active and imaginative warm-up to allow students to review and re-engage with the story of the play through movement.

Preparation and Materials

Space to move

Music

Instructions

1. Create open space in the room (clear of obstacles) with two distinct ends of the room that students can travel to and from.

2. Start the warm-up with a short prompt: "Eagleseye has a map to a hidden box that will save the village from an enemy, and you (the students) are about to join Bentboy on his quest to retrieve the mystery box to save the village!"

3. Give students prompts to the scenes or settings below and ask them to move from one side of the space showing this part of the play with their physical movement.

   ∞ Cross the room imagining you are tiptoeing through a 3-inch deep creek of water. Careful, the rocks might be slippery… now try hopping across the creek instead.

   ∞ Climb the hill that the stone people live on. It is very steep…push and pull with the stone people.

   ∞ Walk against the cold wind blowing snow at you. Lean into the wind. Take shelter to wait out the storm. Then cross easily in the morning.

   ∞ Half of the class: Imagine you are being sucked down into the tree roots. Try to walk away slowly. Roll down slowly.

Other half of the class: Chop at the tree roots, grab Bentboy's hand and pull Bentboy up.

   ∞ Find the box and return it to the village. The creek has grown into a river and you and a partner need to build a raft and paddle across it.

   ∞ You made it back to the village! Celebrate your return with a favourite dance!

Extensions

1. Ask half the group to move and half the group to be an audience. Then switch. Offer opportunities for discussion by having the audience describe the movement they saw. Then offer opportunities for the movers to share what they were representing in the story through their movement.

2. Offer opportunities for students to travel across the room on their own if they are comfortable.